she returns
to the
floating world

JEANNINE HALL GAILEY

Two Sylvias Press

She Returns to the Floating World

Copyright © Jeannine Hall Gailey
July 2011

Two Sylvias Press
P.O. Box 1524
Kingston, WA 98346

www.twosylviaspress.com

Printed in USA
First printing in 2011

ISBN-13: 9780615956800
Library of Congress Control Number: 2011923596

Front cover painting: Rene Lynch, "A Different Sleep" from the Secret Life of the Forest series, oil on canvas, 24" x 48." Courtesy of the artist and Jenkins Johnson Gallery, NYC.

Interior artwork: Michaela Eaves

Author photo, back cover: K. Balasingam

Second Edition

DEDICATION

I'd like to dedicate this book to all my muses:

- My little brother, Michael Duke Hall, whose love of the Japanese language and culture inspired me to study it in the first place.
- My husband, Glenn Allen Gailey, for his patience and love as I worked on this book.
- Gifted director Hayao Miyazaki, whose films have inspired so many.
- Jungian scholar Hayao Kawai, because without his book, many of these poems would not have been possible.
- And, the professor who taught my little brother Japanese, Dr. Ayako Ogawa, and her family, whose invaluable comments helped make this book what it is.

This is a special dedication. It's being written only days after the earthquake and tsunami have wreaked their devastation on Japan. Japan, a country whose folktales repeat the warnings of the dangers of tsunamis and earthquakes throughout generations, whose pop-culture and ancient art display such an intense awareness of apocalypse, of catastrophe. And yet, still, I am caught by surprise, left breathless with sadness at the scope of the tragedy, and praying for hope, for grace, for safety.

The brave Perigee
moon who pulls
the sea too close
is not afraid to show his face
while I hide my own in my
hands and weep.

ACKNOWLEDGMENTS

I would like to say thank you to all the people who gave me valuable feedback and encouragement while I was writing this book:

Pattiann Rogers, Marvin Bell, Sandra Alcosser, Aimee Nezhukumatathil, Dorianne Laux, Joseph Millar, Dr. Ayako Ogawa and her family, Michael Duke Hall, Natasha K. Moni, Jenifer Lawrence, Tom C. Hunley, Lana Hechtman Ayers, Janet N. Knox, Ronda Broatch, Terri Windling, Midori Synder, Roland Kelts, Rusty Childers, and Felicity Shoulders. Thank you all for your time and your support.

I would like to thank my wonderful editors Kelli Russell Agodon and Annette Spaulding-Convy at Two Sylvias Press, and also the original editors of the first edition of the book, the great Anne Petty and Lynn Holschuh at Kitsune Books. Thanks to Rene Lynch for allowing us to use her beautiful work on the cover. Thanks to my talented friend, artist Michaela Eaves, who created the art inside the pages of this book.

I would also like to thank Washington State's Artist Trust GAP grant program, Centrum's residency program, and the Dorothy Sargent Rosenberg Prize for giving me the support I needed to work on this manuscript.

And, of course, thanks to my husband and family.

I would also like to acknowledge the following books and sources as invaluable to my research:

- *The Japanese Psyche: Major Motifs in the Fairy Tales of Japan* by Hayao Kawai
- *Japanamerica: How Japanese Pop Culture Has Invaded the U.S.* by Roland Kelts
- *Anime from Akira to Howl's Moving Castle, Updated Edition: Experiencing Contemporary Japanese Animation* by Susan J. Napier
- *The Fox and the Jewel: Shared and Private Meanings in Contemporary Japanese Inari Worship* by Karen A. Smyers
- *The Endicott Studio of Mythic Arts* website
- *Green Willow and Other Japanese Fairy Tales* by Grace James
- *The Girl Who Loved Caterpillars*, adapted by Jean Merrill

I'd like to gratefully acknowledge all the journals where these poems first appeared.

- "She Returns to the Floating World" parts I, II, and III were published in *Goblin Fruit.*
- "The Kind of Fire of Foxes," "Don't Take Me To the Fireworks, the Fox-Wife Asks," and "The Warning Signs He Should Have Paid Attention to" were published in *Lady Churchill's Rosebud Wristlet.*
- "Jin-Roh: Wolves in Human Armor" appeared in *Strange Horizons.*
- "Married Life" appeared in *Ninth Letter.*
- "The Girl With No Hands" appeared in *Rufous City Review.*
- "Yume (the Dream)" appeared in *32 Poems.*

- "Love Letter to Hayao Miyazaki" was a finalist for the 2007 Beullah Rose Poetry Prize and appeared in *Smartish Pace*.

- "When Asked Why I Write About Japanese Mythology" appeared in *Redactions* and was nominated for the Pushcart Prize. This poem is titled "Postcard from the Suburbs of Seattle..." in this book.

- The haiku "August sky..." won an Honorable Mention in the 2008 Mainichi Haiku Contest in Japan.

- "Winter Etude (with Playstation Accompaniment)" was a finalist in the 2007 Erskine J. Poetry Prize and appeared in *Smartish Pace*.

- "Code" was published in *Sentence: A Journal of Prose Poetics*.

- "The Note the Fox-Wife Leaves Him" appeared in *RHINO*.

- "My Little Brother Learns Japanese" was published in *Calyx*.

- The poems "Dogwood" and "He Makes Dinner" won the top 2007 Dorothy Sargent Rosenberg Prize for Poetry and were published on their site.

- "Advice Before My Wedding" appeared in *Rattle*.

- "Waiting at the OB/Gyn for the Results of a Biopsy" was published in *5 AM*.

- "The Woman Disappears" and "When the Bush-Warbler Returns" appeared in *2River View*.

- "The Fox-Wife's Invitation" appeared in the Spring/ Summer 2008 issue of *The Journal of Mythic Arts*.

- "Yuki, The Snow Maiden," "Green Willow Wife," and "The Tongue-Cut Sparrow" appeared in

Poemeleon. "The Tongue-Cut Sparrow" was nominated for a *Dwarf Star Award.*

- "Uzurazuki (The Month of Quail)" appeared in the San Diego Ink Anthology, *A Year in Ink, Volume 2.*

- "Autobiography" appeared in *Barn Owl Review.*

- "Amaterasu, the Sun Goddess, Returns" appeared in *Poetry International.*

- "The Fox-Wife Describes Their Courtship" appeared in *The Columbia Poetry Journal.*

- "In the Month of Quail" appeared in *Contemporary Haibun Online.*

- "White Bird Sister: Chu Revisits the Past" appeared in the Endicott Studio's *Journal of Mythic Arts.*

- "They Wish Godzilla a Happier Ending" appeared in *Poemeleon.*

- "Love Story (with Fire Demon and Tengu)" appeared in *Cranky* and was republished on "Haibun Today."

- "The Husband Tries to Write to the Disappearing Wife" appeared in *Redactions.*

- "She Likes to Pull Things Apart" appeared in *Wicked Alice.*

- "Standing in the Anime Kingdom" was published in *Siren.*

Table of Contents

Part Three

Part Four

Part One—The Fox-Wife: Come, Love, Sleep

"...a vixen often visited this house and met a man...her husband. She had remembered his words. So, she stayed at night with him. Since then, this woman was named kitsune (*ki-tsu-ne*) which meant 'come, love, sleep.'"

—From a translation by Niji Fuyuno of an 8th-century poem, "The Man Who Married a Vixen" collected in the *Nihon Ryoiki*

The Fox-Wife Dreams

My husband says*, can't trust foxes, their eyes like geodes.*
The wind brings red fur in my window, and the smell of
them clings to my sheets. At the shrine of Inari, he rescued
me. I see in his face he will leave me, the fox tail beneath
my bed clothes betraying. He swears he didn't know I was
kitsune, though my sharp glances were everywhere,
jumping when the dogs bayed. The brown silk robes of my
youth, the smell of smashed leaves underfoot wherever I
walked. The curl beneath the bedsheets. Foxfire, foxflare,
foxfur. Our noses were flames in the forests. The light of
torn paper lanterns is never true, the moonlight uneven. He
always praised my face, the narrow nose, high cheekbones,
close-set eyes. My hair red even when I brushed it darker.

Come sleep with me,
he asked, even after.
Stay with me.

Far away, a fox barking at good fortune. *Faithful, faithful*,
the vixen snaps at his ankles, the taste of rust in the mouths
of our charmed children.

She Likes To Pull Things Apart

The tissue-thin layers of a croissant,
the yolks of eggs, the membrane
skins of pomegranates, all
more delicious when displayed.

In class she dissected pigs,
loved cracking the jaw,
the incision from the corner
of the mouth to neckline,
the beautiful tongue laid out.

In med school she sliced
through cartilage of cadavers,
then struggled to break open
the rib cage to observe
the heart within, how each is molded.

She scratches at your shoulder
the way she scratches a lime's skin,
to burst the cells beneath her nails.
She bites an ear lobe or the blunt tips
of fingers, your lower lip and thigh.
She splinters ice in her teeth between kisses.

Crane Wife

My husband, you have forgotten
how many bolts of cloth I wove for you
the children I bore you, the nights
I lay by your side to warm you.

When you were poor, you gave all you had
to buy the life of a white crane.
You loved her then. And when
I came to you dressed in white,

you did not recognize me,
agreed to be my husband, and all I asked
was for you not to look at me bathing,
when my true nature might be revealed.

(You would wake up with feathered
remnants on your hands and face,
rinsing them with cold water. Was this
a dream, you wondered.)

You have asked for more,
you have opened the closet door;
I flew away, a crane who had given you
her white glory, and you knew the cloth

to be the sacrifice of my own skin, my feather coat.
A thousand cranes descended on your hut,
crying with betrayal. You searched all of Japan for me
until you found a lake of cranes, those white ciphers,

cried your goodbyes, useless, now, with age.
You had the gift of my wings, knew the lift
of flight and the gentle neck. Now, old man,
remember, when you watch a flash in the sky,

remember me, remember

The Fox-Wife Describes Their Courtship

I had given up the world, given my body to death or any
possible rebirth. When he found me at the shrine of Inari,
I became something else. But when the smoke rose, it was
still me, terrified, turning and turning from the heat.
How could he quiet this new body, its voices and tears?
When we're alone, I forget my other life sometimes, forget
my sharp teeth and tail. I become the thing beneath his
hands, softer.

We all wear our voices out calling for each other, and
when does that song end? He loved the falling cherry
blossoms, the crumpling peonies, the dying willow. He
always sought to put things back together. I tear things
apart. The instruments of bone and blood are the same;
the intents are different. I look down and see my paw on
his hand. He sees the half-moons of nails, the pink skin.
He sees the hope in changing seasons, and I only see
the leaves departed, the savage inky trails of the moon
in the grass.

I know before he does
how he will leave me,
a little temple of spine and fur.

Advice Given to Me Before My Wedding

Better to be the lover than the beloved, you'll have passion.
Better to be the beloved, a sure thing, a lifetime of that.

He is more beautiful but you,
you have more power. Which is to say,

you are just like your brother. Lift your eyes
and people do what you say. Who knows why.

Men are like breakfast cereal. You have to pick one.
Fish in the sea, a dime a dozen. They are singing for you, now.

Keep your own bank account. Keep working.
Give him a blowjob, and he'll volunteer to take out the trash.

You are mine, says the beloved, and I am yours.
Whither you go I will go. Honey and milk are under her tongue.

Cancer and Taurus, very compatible.
You're the hard-charger, he's the homemaker.

Don't stop wearing lipstick. Don't put on any weight.
Don't buy the dress too soon. If you go on the pill,
    your breasts will swell.

One day you might regret. You might do better.
You could do worse. One man's as good as another.

Wear my old pearls. Here's the blue, a handkerchief
embroidered with tears. If you won't wear heels, you'll
    look short in the pictures.

If you don't wear a veil, people will say you're not a virgin.
Good luck, glad tidings, a teddy, a toaster. So long, farewell.

Postcard from the Suburbs of Seattle to the Suburbs of Tokyo

I will send my voices out over the water
where the same cedars that litter my coast
used to tower over yours. Once green,
your cities have nibbled forests into bonsai.

Our hinoki trees are shipped across the ocean
for your sacred temples now.
Postcards of volcanoes rise from a blue sky

in the background of our homes, we share
zones of tsunami, seasons of weeping cherry.

I read about women's spirits
haunting peony lanterns in the forest.
Men follow them, fall in love
with women long dead. In shallow graves
rotted with tree roots, they still sing.

And here in pages hammered
from your language into mine,
sometimes with clumsy fists,
I have listened to the bush-warbler
mourn her children, the fox-wife's eyes
in the darkness have warned me
of the growling of dogs and fire.

And when they disappear in silence,
it is not really silence. Their echoes
burn themselves into stone,
into the living screens of my childhood,
fill my mouth with ghosts.

Ghosts sit in my mouth and sing.
Our grandfathers were at war.

I grew up in the birthplace
of bombs that poisoned children,
burned holes into your sacred earth.
Their poison is part of me.

In the shelter of a shrine, a small girl
holds an umbrella. She becomes a white bird.
She whispers and a thousand cranes,
a thousand burning flowers
pile up inside me, spill out onto these pages.

Forgive me, ghosts, for my hard,
unbeautiful hands, for my tripping tongue,
as you demand a healed future, some untorn prayer.

In the Month of Quail

The shoes I am wearing bruise the top of my feet. On our
trail there are rabbits and waxwings, a heron in the stream,
exotic loud swans. Stomping through the grass I discover
my quail, now he's become six—the father and mother,
four crownless children. Why had he been calling at my
window? Was he calling for her, his mate, his children?
Isolated from family, solitary, a state foreign to quail?
Quail stand for togetherness in dreams, because, as you
see, they hoot to each other, they shake together as one
covey, they wander up through the thicket, calling out in
the blackberries.

He stands guard,
proudly. They are round
like little fall fruits.

Where will these quail lead me? Already the dusk is
following, the swallows are becoming bats in the August
darkness. Beware of sitting alone in your little house, he
tells me from the thorny branches, beware of listening too
long to the calls of tear-shaped birds, using them for
guidance.

Amaterasu, The Sun Goddess, Withdraws

I cannot give you
what you want, what you wanted
me to become.
I cannot gather your fragments,
revive you with gold breath.

My limbs are splattered
with the mud of my garden,
detritus of trees.
What fingers I have cannot
stir you now, I have lost laughter.

I have lost hope. While
my brother (the moon, the storm)
takes over heaven,
or what you imagined
heaven to be. The animals

have all hidden
underground, to be nearer
to me. I will not
come out until I have borne
a new laughter, and that will not be

for centuries. I shield
my eyes from you, the dirty
earth, and my own
reflection. Neither of us
can read what the future holds:

my face on your flag,
the bodies dying,
dying in my name.
The burning. The flash.
The desolation of atoms.

Horoscope

Chinese Horoscope: Born 1973, the Year of the Ox –
Sincere, persevering, stubborn, intelligent.
Born in April under Taurus the Bull:
headstrong, material, another working stiff.

But how can a horoscope say anything about you?
laughing, he asks me. *Can everyone born*
in the same week, in the same year, have the same traits?
Ridiculous, he shrugs, *even to suggest it.*

But here I am, weighted down by my intractable
horns, pushing you out of your shell, little Crab, little Cancer,
as we build a nest from earth and water.

August Sky

August sky
    a quail's cry softens
        blackberry thorns

Anime Girl Delays Adulthood

She may or may not have burned down her school,
but you know she likes to strike matches,
throw them in a circle around her,
pray to some unknown god of fire.

Broken, you think, she must be in high school,
her skirt is too short, her hair still in pigtails,
feeding stray cats and playing video games
under a bridge. You watch her rinse out her socks.

Barefoot in the water, her lips pursed,
she peruses her surroundings, surreptitiously
sneaking shots of the ruined warehouse
in the distance with a camera. An eerie glow on the
horizon.

You wish her the best. You hope she leaves and never comes back.
You hope for a kiss, a sandwich. A burned thumb.
You were never right for her; she was always on the lookout
for an easy out, the last train to nowhere, the final frame.

Part Two — Rescuing the Blue Dragon

"The patriarchal social system that prevailed in Japan until the end of World War II obscured our eyes. . .In fairytales, however, "female heroes" could freely take an active part. The investigation of those female figures will cast light on the psyche of the Japanese."

—Hayao Kawai, from his book,
The Japanese Psyche:
Major Motifs in the Fairy Tales of Japan

An American Love Letter to Hayao Miyazaki

We don't understand
the Shinto symbols—ears shaped
like temple points or

Phurba daggers on
one animal, a "no-face"
mask on another.

In your movies, stone
dogs stand watch in the background,
and children lean

against them, crying.
Here, pets and disposable
cameras do not

come with *kami*-spirits;
we do not see the dragons
in our rivers, gleaming.

But we know where you
lead us, on your kite-powered
airships, over the valleys

on fire and mushrooming
treetops, we know we are trying
to find the Japan

of your childhood,
the green tips of rice against
the blue open air,

your boy-fear, the dark
menacing clouds you watched rise
over your country.

My Little Brother Learns Japanese
—For Mike, *Watashi wa otouto ga daisuki desu.*

In college, he learns to read
right to left,
practicing with *Manga*,
learns *Kanji* picture-words:
how the word for *heart*
can also mean *indigo blue*.

He learns to conjugate
verbs with no future,
and reads poetry that does not
begin with "I."

He learns about weather reports
of *sakura zensen,*
the advance of cherry-blossom fronts
and finds that falling blossoms
can also mean dead soldiers.

He knows the word for *bird*
by its feet, and knows
a *village* connects hands to trees.
Little brother is a student,
and *older sister*
is a woman going to the city.

He learns in Japanese fairy tales
that siblings, not spouses,
are often saviors;
the older sister brings the dead brother
back to life
over and over again.

The Princess Who Loved Insects

In the brief, beeless January sunlight
I climb, bareheaded, through the trees
to find a nest of caterpillars, fuzzy and striped
that I hide in my kimono sleeves.

My mother wails in the darkened house
because I won't shave my eyebrows
or blacken my teeth, am not anxious
about the sun. My father shakes his head, and sighs.

Other girls dance with the butterflies
who flutter through the gardens, brilliant,
but they fear the silkworms' writhing,
who weave their clothing, silent.

In the sea a blue dragon dances. No one sees
but me and my tiny allies.
I know each summer my feet grow
longer and more brown

as I watch the pupae harden,
split and glisten—
as I, too, wait to be wrapped, stilled,
in layers of silk.

The Taste of Rust in August

Knoxville afternoons in summer, lightning on the air.
The horses whinny, nervous; the chickens roost.

Our chain-link fence is rusty. I like to taste it—
that metallic clean I imagine to be the flavor

of lightning. My brother was hit once, carrying
a metal bucket to water the animals. It burned

his arm, and left a funny taste in his mouth.
Mother says I have always sucked on spoons,

licked lampposts, iron grates, jewelry.
She goes crazy about the germs.

She says I do it because of what she calls *iron-poor blood*
and it's true—there's no rust in my skin at all,

dull and transparent as wax paper.
I run around the yard for hours, chasing the lightning,

tracing those fractal lines in the sky with my fingers
as the smell of ozone drives the dogs crazy.

Rescuing Seiryu, the Blue Dragon

You met the dragon in the garden. Sometimes he flies in
circles outside your window. This morning he appeared as
a young boy. He shows you a vision of your parents, lying
in a barn. With his face so close you smell hay.

He bleeds from the wounds of paper birds, from a
swallowed curse. Can your healing rice cake keep him
from death? You hold his head in your arms as he squirms
red, you force his jaws open and touch his teeth. When you
feed him he gags and chokes, changing from human to
dragon and back, his eyes always blue.

The dragon is really the river of your childhood home. He
hands you a pink tennis shoe you lost in the water when
you were seven. That river was drained years ago for
development.

Since then the dragon
has no home but you, no name
but your memory.

Code

My brother and I were sickly, pale kids, apt to bleed easily
at a scratch from a dog's claw or tree branch, vomiting and
hives from too much grass and sunlight. Happier in our
pillow fort caves, poring over comic book panels and fairy
tale woodcuts. Miyazaki's Anime—we join magic hang
glider flights over poisoned forests, gas masks, protective
gloves, a world of giant caterpillars with eerie songs,
molds and spores that sear flesh. *This* made sense, our
pixilated metaphor, the girl in the pictures saves everyone.

The boy and girl can
hide in crystalline underground
forests of mineral.

*

Code II

Because in childhood we imagine ourselves fierce, super-
powered mutants so different we must become heroes.
Because now my little brother teaches Shao Lin Do to tiny
would-be monks, displaying the dragon, the monkey.
Because still in my dreams I am gliding like a kite over
dangerous, diseased tree branches, safe in my enchanted
consort with caterpillars.

*

Code III

When I turn twenty, the boys are so grateful I speak the
language of their childhoods they invite me to midnight
screenings of sci-fi flicks, tell me their secret government

hacks. At night there are robots, Godzilla, our thumbs
grow numb killing zombies together.
I get to be the blue-haired waif in silk with a scimitar and
the blonde in a white bikini. Because I know the code.
Code for something broken. Code of ephemeral DNA.
Code for "you too can become heroes," for ambition,
greatness.

Code for heaven.
Code that spells out messages of love
only you understand.

The Princess and Her Swan Brothers

My father made a casket for each son
so I might inherit the kingdom
all I could do was pick nettles, nettles
shirts for my swan siblings
I lived in a cave and a king found me
I would not speak and he took me to a castle
but all I would do was weave nettles, nettles
I could not speak a word and then
my brothers the swans visit me at night
weep tears on blistered fingers

If I speak they will be birds forever
the king wanted me for his bride
I could not speak
his people tried to burn me
my hands full of nettles and feathers
I wept but could not speak
The flames startle upwards
my brothers your shirts made of nettles, here
in the sky seven swans circled the village crying
and the swans flew out of the sky human
I opened my mouth to speak
the sound like air rushing through white feathers

Girl with Kit Fox: A Scene

At the edge of a clearing in Cades Cove. She's carefully
watching a kit fox in the grass, making its way towards
her. She doesn't know whether to run or offer her hand.
The girl and the fox eye each other warily. There is a smell
of grain in the air, the early sunlight making everything
more yellow. A few yards away, a bird startles and the fox
turns its attention to a cricket in the warm dirt.

Red fur, red clay
a young girl doing her best to be still
the snap of teeth.

Wild Strawberries and Anime Fires

When I was little in Tennessee, a neighbor shook his gun
in my father's face. Later this man would burn down his
own house. We did not understand the spite of a man who
would destroy himself to hurt those around him. But
Miyazaki's pictures were full of these fires, waves of
them, consuming trees and mountains, razing village after
village. What kind of fire came from the hearts of men?
He was trying to show us the rage of a dying king who
would use the children of his people like a shield against
fires he had started himself. A country devoured
by such fires. And the things that grow from the ground of
such destruction. The children with burn scars on their
arms grew up and planted trees; one such child grew up
and painted the world again, a world where the spirits did
not hide their faces.

The tiny strawberries
that grew above the burned house
were the sweetest I ever tasted.

Oak Ridge Haiku

The wasps and swallows
                build nests from radioactive mud
                        in a neighbor's house.

Big Sister, Little Brother

I brought you back to life
but first, I had to become you:
dress up in your clothes,
track down your enemies
and make them eat
their own poisoned rice.

It wasn't the first time
I saved you from your
so-called friends; before
the deadly banquet,
there was a fan contest,
when I made you a fan
of living bush-warblers,
and a boat contest,
the boat I built you
rowed to shore by magic clay dolls.

Over and over I saved you,
but this time, taking your place
among the shocked faces at the table,
I realized how small a thing
it would be to slip into your life:
the school, the friendships,
the easy path. For a moment,
my feet could cover more ground,
and my strong fingers and jaw
were assets. I've never been jealous

of anything but this. As I gather
a thousand flowers to burn
and pray to the gods to revive you,
I will not begrudge you anything,
little brother—take the gold of my hands,
the river of my breath—
walk among the living,

with my straight eyebrows and long calves.

Be strong in a land seeking to destroy us,
and for one of us, at least,
my magic will be enough.

Dogwood

I grew up with uneven
petals of dogwood
not the pink faces of cherry blossoms—
not the wide white faces of magnolia—
not skunk cabbages or plum branches.
Tough and twisted branches grafted last winter
lifted me up.

And you wonder how
I grew this knotty, beauty
burned at the edges,
blooming before my leaves
even caught the light?

In the Anime Version of My Life

I fight a blue dragon with a sword that grows from my
arm. In battle I glow with a bright light. My pink dress is
soaked by the blood of giant caterpillars. I walk on a field
of antennae. I've hidden a garden of poisonous dandelions
in the secret passageways of the castle. I wear a flying
squirrel on my shoulder like a talisman. My skirt floats up
in the wind of airborne ships. I slice through handcuffs of
captured princesses and rescue men riding flightless birds.
I send packages home to my brother full of magic seeds,
scrolls containing secret messages and healing rice cakes.
In the forest I meet demons and try to stop their blood with
my hands, but instead I become part of their rage.

I eat the venom
from dead enemies and become
a ghost figure

feared by the villagers. The villagers are steel workers
rescued from prostitution and men with broken teeth and
missing hands. I want to help them but they keep hunting
the spirit wolves, they don't understand the wolf and the
boar and their own hearts are the same. They shoot me and
stab me with knives, they tear down the trees that anchor
their city. I will become their unrecognizable savior, the
one they worshipped in stories written on old tapestry, the
one the old women have told them about. All the colors
will be fluid and springlike, my eyes will be luminous as
the skin of butterflies, everyone will pray
for my limp figure to be revived.

White Bird Sister

Little brother, you watched our stepmother
boil me in a pot, thought you had lost me.
You found a white bird

who brought you cedar branches,
wove you gold clothing.
We had told father to remarry, we trusted and lost.

So you go with your stepsister
to my husband, the prince.
She wears my veil, you call her Chu, my name.

In the forests you are lonely, you call
and I visit as a white bird. (Carry on, Carry on.)
In the palace you sleep in the fire grate.

You are found by the prince
who has married my stepsister in my name.
The false Chu is killed.

You fill carthenware bowls with water for me.
When the sun rises,
you pull me from the King of the next world,

back to my buried body.
I return to you.
I marry my rightful husband.

I'll protect you, watch over you
in this world and the next.
Never fear, little brother,

that the white bird will forget.
Keep to your prayers and I will find you.
Carry on, Carry on.

Holiday Redux

This is family—it is fourteen below outside and you find a
bruise on your shin where your brother kicked you. There
are leftovers in the fridge and a thousand lumpy,
mismatched cookies on a plate with a green napkin. In
fifteen minutes you will lie down on a bed swaybacked
from generations of bodies, bodies freakishly immune to
their own daisy-wheeled minutes. In your hands are the
wrappers to candy, presents, the bones of chickens.
Sometimes in the night you hear scratching at the window,
you wonder if you're being attacked by wolves.

In your dreams
you are facedown in a puddle,
struggling to breathe.

Yume (The Dream)

You were flying in circles outside my window, yowling
into the air. Blue blood dribbled from your mouth, and
your claws were broken. Why can't I lead you to the right
song, the right garden? Where the butterflies left their
cocoons on the grass. Where there seemed to be silence.
When you told me you felt wrong, I should have believed.

I keep spinning in the green air, faces in the trees. I should
have found a light to lead us home, should have followed
the glow of the peony lantern. One more basket to fill, one
more path to abandon. Promise you won't quit, promise
you won't leave your feet where others could trample
them. I will leave your clothing in a woven basket, I will
cover myself in feathers so you will not recognize me.

If you sing to the pines,
for a few days I will answer,
then no more.

I must marry the king of the spirit world. I must leave you
behind however you howl.

Part Three — In the Anime Kingdom

"Pop culture is now part of our unconscious. Writers descend into themselves . . . what they often encounter in their own deeper psyche are fragments of TV programs they saw as kids, books they read, music they heard . . . . "

— Motoyuki Shibata, from "Look, Here's America"
Spring 2006 issue of *A Public Space*

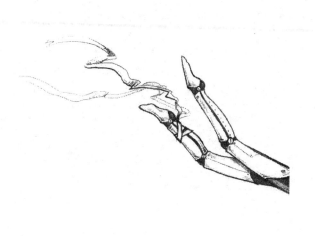

Standing in the Anime Kingdom

A dangerous wonderland—
too many fruit and me without my minikilt,
surrounded by minigirls whose minitops
are falling off, their eyes too big.

Surrounded by tall men, Otaku,
mocking the American dub,
who thumb through Manga,
read stories of half-wolf demon boys,
kids imprisoned in robot bodies
and vampire princesses—
even a female cyborg in a thong.

I am afraid, all these child-like faces
pressed up against the pages
like they want to get out.
Here in this kingdom
I lean into the glass, distorted, wide-eyed.

I have left my fox ears behind,
too heavy beneath the weight of these boys and their
candy-colored hallucinations,
hear Ragnarok and cyberpunks
thwack their tiny battles beneath my fingertips.

O, where are you Nausicaa,
you rescuer of Odysseus,
playing your harp instead of lessons?
Where are you, princess of caterpillars?

Chaos Theory

Elbow-deep in the guts of tomatoes,
I hunted genes, pulling strand from strand.
DNA patterns bloomed like frost.

Ordering chaos was my father's talisman;
he hated imprecision, how in language—
the word is never exactly the thing itself.

I remembered him speaking
about the garden of the janitor
at the Fernald Superfund site,

Mutations burgeoned in fractal branchings.
The dahlias and tomatoes he showed to my father,
doubling and tripling in size and variety,

magentas, pinks and red so bright they blinded,
churning offspring gigantic and marvelous
from that ground sick with uranium.

The janitor smiled proudly. My father nodded,
unable to translate for him the meaning
of all this unnatural beauty.

In his mind he watched the man's DNA
unraveling, patching itself together again
with wobbling sentry enzymes.

When my father brought this story home,
he never mentioned the janitor's radiation poisoning,
only those roses, those tomatoes.

They Wish Godzilla a Happier Ending

Dragon who arrives from the sea, your breath melts
skyscrapers and your tiny hands wave piteously. In the city
they chant your name, a mantra, a prayer, hoping the sea
might bring more than destruction. You lift yourself from
the water, feet planted square on bus tracks and shopping
malls. O lizard of psychic remembrance, O dragon,
dinosaur, our angered water spirit, you may also become a
protector. You bat pterodactyls away from the city with
one hand, stop the flames of a turtle with another. Your
hands like decaying sea-flowers. You roar as if hurt, your
mouth horrible, your atomic breath a curse you cannot end.
Your dreams are filled always with acrid smoke, decaying
charred rubble, the skeletons of school children, and you
want them to stop. Swim away into the nuclear glow of
sunset, O Godzilla, whose skin matches the mossy tide, to
a gentler ending, away from the island of sorrows,
tsunamis, away from miniature maidens and soldiers
wobbling, as if unsure, as they watch you go.

The green water flows
trickling from knees and ankles
as your breathing slows.

Aberrant Code I

So many aberrations in the code.
I watch a show about mutant heroes, evolution.
My doctor asked if I had powers like the X-Men.
When I woke up with one broken heart
and all the crashing blood, your face was gold.
You would never know from looking how
un-human I am. They are always trying to touch me.
I push them away, try to explain how my animal-self
is different than theirs. They never listen.
Try Again Later, the machine tap taps.
So small these animal parts, one giant cosmic swirl,
a swarm of bees. The x-rays confuse radiologists.
I can't even locate myself on this map.

The Lost Limbs of Anime Girls in Space

Somehow in these futuristic worlds
we have always left an arm
and a leg behind, as if these amputations
make us seem more accessible,

a portion of our torsos beneath the torn top
visible—a glimpse of shining silver.
Our hair still charmingly tousled,
we are victims of some civil war

or village atrocity conveniently unwritten,
forgotten now, military campaigns hidden in our pasts.
Only these reminders that we might not be
entirely human—merely a ghost

caught in a metal shell. *She'll give you
an arm and a leg,* they joke, while we
wake in the night to scratch phantom skin,
the joints between flesh and machine always aching,

our souls affixed in some permanent alchemy
to this heavy metal.

A Grownup Considers the Spiritual Themes
of a Children's Movie
(or, Relating Miyazaki's *My Neighbor Toto*ro to Psalm 73)

They say it is a camphor tree, camphor
the scent of clean lungs, unscarred
by Tokyo smog, TB, the smoke of American bombs.

And I am here looking for hope.
There it is, round, unintelligible,
on top of the camphor tree.

If I prayed right now to the spirit of this tree,
would he appear?
Would I cling to his furry belly
and would he carry me to the treetops,
whistling through a gourd?

> *When I was little, I thought "When I am 21,*
> *I will not be afraid of shots."*
> *I was hiding under a table.*
> *And it was true, a good thing,*
> *since there would be so many needles*
> *after twenty, carrying blood that ran too fast*
> *away into tiny vials, labeled*
> *with indecipherable letters and numbers.*

If we waited by a tree in the dark,
would we be rescued? Would the kami-spirit
of the forest watch over a little girl in the dark?

She is crying. It's late, and raining.
The leaves are her umbrella.
In the fearful grip of absence we squeeze our souls

for some reassurance. Are you there, God?
Is there balm in Gilead?
Will you make of me a threshing sledge?
The hospital lights are so cold. I'm afraid.

In my dreams a spirit appears. It welcomes me.
I am twelve again, and it pats my hair.
It laughs in the rain, at the rain, at the sound of rain.

So many nights in the hospital.
Next to me through the curtain someone is
moaning,
someone is hitting the nurse.
Police stroll through the corridors.
I murmur prayers, My flesh and my heart may fail,
but god is the strength . . .
though I tried to understand,
it was too difficult for me.
If I had spoken,
I would have betrayed your children . . .

Is it possible to tumble through the clearing to find you,
though we were not seeking?
Is it possible to pull your tail,
will you breathe your name into our ears?
Will you give us acorns to plant,
will you let us fly on the wind?
Will you watch over us,
will you live in a camphor tree?

The little girl rests on a shrine made of stone.
In the morning, the statue is covered with acorns.

By the hospital window, you watch from a branch,
eyes glowing, until we fall asleep.

Aberrant Code II

If you had known early on I could speak
to the animals because I have been there,
in the dust, that my fingers were familiar
with grass and leaves and even the spiders
understood. I ate the grass and prayed
to become another being, but I was already
blessed with DNA so sampled, broken
that no one could relay its message.
Underneath the grass and snow: the bodies
of nuclear bombs. Spring whispers
but the fish grow limbs in the light.
In my dreams I sail through wind, fight with swords.
In this body trapped beneath the layers of skin
some strange worm, some dragon, some other soul.

Little Girls, Atom Bombs

Miyazaki draws an angel rising
from Chernobyl's coffin. Men with hazmat suits
keep her in a secret room, with signs warning:
"Stay Out of the Sun" "Life is Not Guaranteed."

Kat grew up near Chernobyl. She tells me
about the mushrooms from her town,
showing up at markets miles to the East,
three-hundred-times-full of the poison from earth.

I grew up in Oak Ridge, all my friends
physicists' daughters, sons of nuclear engineers.
Behind our school, the giant domed houses of bombs.
We played in snow measured with a Geiger counter.

In Seattle, I visit a statue of Sadako, from Hiroshima.
In her hands are dozens of paper cranes, replaced after
rainfall. She believed a thousand paper birds could save
her. A thousand rainbow cranes marked her last birthday, twelve.

We read about nuclear winter, mutated farm animals:
Chernobyl's goats birth tougher, scrubbier versions
of themselves. We discuss eco-saviors in Anime,
become the little girl scrubbing a river spirit with magic herbs.

Will these gods be appeased? Will we stop trees
from growing radioactive fruit? Will a thousand paper
birds fly out of our mouths, carry away each splinter of
poison, each molecule of twisted, irreparable DNA?

Winter Etude
(with Playstation Accompaniment)

Outside porch lights flicker with menace
between the sharp edges of leaves

while Japanese pop music blares
out of a box in the living room.

One more bowl of popcorn
to wear around our necks, around trees

and a dog barks shrilly into the cold
wind. One family member huddles alone

over a laptop, two others pick at leftover
meats, and three more argue the merits

of various ex-girlfriends. Diet Coke bottles
scattered through rooms. Upstairs,

the wrapping paper weeps silently
in wastebaskets, unable to tear themselves

from the memories of hands clutching
frantically, then just as suddenly, silence, the

slow tiring of smiles. One for the road,
one for the New Year, all hope

packed neatly into boxes and suitcase.

Visions from a Futuristic Dystopia - View I

I was waiting
for a robot to explode
on the horizon
but as the camera pans up
my skinny legs
you can see
the horizon oppressive as history
melting over me

Visions from a Futuristic Dystopia - View II

I ride a wolf
clutching a stone dagger
desperate to save someone—
you? me? the generous dawn?
I don't wear lipstick
or the costume you've made for me.
In fact, you can barely hear me breathing
into the light which has already faded,
my history crumbling into fragments,
the red elk going extinct,
the forests of conifers slowly growing smaller
on the outskirts of the city;
still the outline of my shadow
is visible. It grows without your permission.
Someday, the spirits will be on my side.

Part Four — Mono No Awaré

" . . . the feeling of awaré (softly despairing sorrow)
which a Japanese would feel for the female figure who
disappears in silence...It is a Japanese cultural paradigm
that a woman must disappear in order for sorrow to
complete the sense of beauty...The woman is far from
angry with the man when her taboo is broken; she just
vanishes."

—Hayao Kawai, from *The Japanese Psyche:*
Major Motifs in the Fairy Tales of Japan

Inari Speaks

You have forgotten that once I was a woman, not a fox—
once a guardian of grain, of children and swords, now all
of my statues have pointed ears and tails. I came down
from the cold mountains to feed you each spring. Yes, it
was my voice that brought the shoots of rice, the winds of
my breath that stirred them in the sun. I had an army of
foxes that did my bidding, their ghost muzzles in your
dreams, stirring. Leave behind your charms, your flowers
at my shrines on the sides of roads. Dress stone foxes in
red scarves and ask them about your marriages, your dead
sons—they will answer as stone answers. Even now I fade
in your memories, my figure dimming in the lights of your
cities. Whatever you once received from me, I can no
longer give you—I have retreated to the mountains with
my white-furred servants, where I will sleep in the snow
until once again you resurrect me.

After Ten Years Together, We Sneak Off
To Make Out in Someone's Closet

Snuffling, bumping elbows against mops,
hitting our knees at awkward angles,
I squeeze the beeswax candle on accident
instead of you, and you hit your head
on a box of matches, scattering sparks
around us in the dark as we breathe
sweat and dust and the now-familiar soapy taste
of our skins, here amid fly swatters, empty
milk bottles, your back pink and smooth with its knots
of muscle like pulled taffy under my fingertips.
Two blind naked mole rats reaching
closer after ten years of marriage, trying to find
the magnets within us under clavicle, scapula,
hip bone, sternum, that repel and attract us,
the volcanic fissures that separate me from you.

Aberrant Code III

Increasingly alienated. Alien.
Subject: 33, white, female. Dk brown hair, lt eyes.
The terms from there grow foreign.
You wouldn't recognize me in this chart.
So is this some interspecies love song,
you, grown tree-like; me, a fox in the dust,
some hybrid of woman and mythical beast?
The sense of taboo—underneath
all those layers of white nightgown, who knew?
You wear a gold ring beaten from years.
I like to chew jewelry. Your blood plus mine a disaster,
our offspring sinking ships. Anyway, your hair is golden,
just like the fairy tales. So you ought to expect
some hidden chambers, blood on the egg.

Jin-Roh: Wolves in Human Armor

In this false future of Nazi costumes
my friends and I wear gas masks
rendering us unrecognizable on a playground.

We are called a wolf-pack
and you, Red, are nothing but bait
to test my sense of duty.

You resemble a young girl I knew
and failed to kill. They picked you out,
called you a terrorist, ran you ragged.

Named you her sister.
And again, as a dog returns
 you know I will chase you, your basket

of weaponry, your red hood
into the darkness. You will be hurt,
and I, never really the hero,

the one to fire the shot.
Unable to leave the pack, I become
a shadow wolf, gnawing his own leg to bone.

The Fire of Foxes - I

In this parable the foxes are weapons. They run but the fire
on their tails is not imagination. In the dry grasses, the
foxes quickly fizzle to bone in the twilight. The smells of
the fat grain and the glossy olive bark, the foxfur, sting
their noses. Because the father would not hand his
daughter, the man's wife, over, they are both burned by the
villagers. In this parable, the man brings destruction with
foxfire and jawbones. They say it is the spirit of the Lord.
The foxes in the forest cry all night in the outskirts—the
singed bodies of their family and the man's wife lie
together against the mountains. The foxes do not cry out
for justice. They return to their lairs even more wary. Their
flames shall not be used by man again. To burn a warning
into their hearts. To burn.

The Fire of Foxes - II

In another story a man lights a fox on fire to save others, to
warn them of tsunami. The fox is a willing partner,
burning brightly in the night to tell the village and his own
people to flee. The men and foxes see the fire and run. The
water comes and swallows the burning fox, the old farmer
who lit him, and all the farmland. But the families of fox
and man are safe. The rice smolders underwater. The fox
is rewarded with eternal life; his eyes and tail become stars
in the sky. At least that is the version I have learned by
heart.

Yuki, The Snow Maiden

I warned you, my husband,
that night in the snow,
when you saw the deadly power of my kiss,
never to speak of what you witnessed.
You left the old man I'd covered in ice,
returned safe to your mother as I promised.
I showed up on your doorstep,
with another name—
my shining robes discarded,
my white hair blinding black,
and you did not know me.
You mistook my silent lips
and quiet ways for goodness.
We married, our children played
while you wove them sandals
in the house that we shared.
You stayed handsome and I never aged.
But one winter night you spoke,
while watching me sew,
of your dream of a snow woman,
who looked like me in the moonlight,
just as pale. And I cried as I left you
with one chilling gaze.
You never keep our secrets.
The gusts of snow around your window
are all that's left of me—my breath
and my children, who press their cheeks
against the cold ground, who hate the thaw of spring.

Uzurazuki (The Month of Quail)

Wednesday I tried to lie down but couldn't sleep. Outside
it was daylight, I had forgotten my name and who I was. A
quail kept calling, one quail all alone, outside my window.
Was he waiting for me? I knew what day of the week it
was, what outfit I was wearing, but memory is like that
sometimes, water, it slips through. A quail crying alone for
six days. I wish I knew where we were going, this quail
and I. Whether I was going to leap through the window
into some other life. Whether or not I would wake up one
day and suddenly know flight. Follow the clouds away
from here. Follow some dream I can't remember. What did
you say?

The name of the rocks here,
not granite, not limestone. Something
more blue. Agate?

The way you said my name sounded like wings. Maybe I
do have wings. What to remember, the way I made that
sound that sounded like crying, the taste of rust rising in
my throat like wings.

When Asked What Makes Her Unique

Her kidneys are not like butterfly wings,
a symmetrical pairing;
not two tidy red beans
but one long horseshoe,
conjoined twin organs
hugging her together,
hiding her from CAT scans,
from the probes of doctors.

Her heart flutters
out of sync, the press of unseen wings against
ventricles making her pulse
skitter, her lungs lunge
one after the other, working
to pull oxygen from starved blood
that cannot stop itself rushing, rushing.

Blue bruises butterfly beneath her skin
moving like storm clouds
from ankle to thigh;
bruises from brushing against a piece of furniture,
from a too-tight embrace, from pressing a book
too hard to her chest. She mashes a thumb
against her arm to watch the print darken.

Inside her they find a twinned uterus—
no wineskin, no pink balloon—
instead, two palms thrusting out
repeating "No,"
two wings ragged and tired of blood,
interrupting cycles of moon and tide,
two doors closing.

Aberrant Code IV

There have been a lot of needles and blood,
so the faint-hearted should turn away right now.
Talk about mermaids—one hundred years
of love gone awry, my parents two imperfect.
So: digestive, reproductive, systems blunted, unclear,
her blood too thin and lungs more suited for water than air.
I should never enter the hospital, let the doctors look at me
in wonder. I wasn't meant for this fish-tank, this testing hub.
Who cares what you're like underneath?
We don't fall in love with what we peel under skin.
You said, don't ask me if I'd do it again.
I said, I'd be happier under glass.

Green Willow Wife

I begged you not to take me far
from home, I was so young, my black hair
uncut and unbound, loose over your hands, my feet bare
while I poured you warm sake by the fire.

We roamed villages, me in the foamy green clothing
you bought for my thin legs and shoulders.
I'm so tired, I'll die, I told you. I lay down
on the wet grass beside the river. How I loved you,

my husband, do not forget your green willow.
In the morning, all that was left of me
was my green silk scarf and skirt
and a sheaf of green willow leaves.

When you went back to my village, grieving,
the three willow trees in front of my house
cut down, and the house itself decayed,
my parents missing . . . Poor husband,

you should have known the green willow
could not stray far. Let me lie down on the grass.
Let the rain fall on the stumps of my soul.
Remember the green willow,

who gave you her young limbs,
with whom you lay on white wooden mats.

He Wonders What, Exactly, He Rescued

His hands are full of brambles, and the woman
in that tower a bit more feral than anticipated;
it turns out she had a bone collection
and a habit of turning princes into toads.
With her hair cut short, sometimes her eyes
and cheekbones look so sharp she reminds him
of some forest creature gone astray in a floating green dress.
He makes dinner for the two of them,
gently snapping asparagus in two, cutting
the fascia away from a chicken breast with a sigh.
A backfire, a black spire, a fear ark, a fae bicker:
a creature with a beautiful song and sharp claws.
Nothing the way he'd pictured it.

He Makes Dinner

The thick knife gleams under your strong hands,
slicing carrot, onion, garlic, pepper,
scattering slivers into the air,
staining your fingers with their gold juices.
You chop so quickly the definite line
between "hand" and "knife" dissolves.
You strew pieces into the skillet,
listen for the right sting and sizzle of oil and wine,
waiting to feed me the work of your hands,
that broken finger, the tiny cuts
that lace and scar your surfaces.

Love Story (with Fire Demon and Tengu)

Maybe in this version you are a bird, and I have become an
old woman. Maybe you ate a falling star. It's hard to love
someone in a castle—they always feel distant. I will open
a flower shop and learn to speak German, take to wearing
ruffled dresses and straw hats. You'd like to pin me down,
but you could tell my feet weren't touching the ground. I
called your name over and over, but you couldn't hear me
above the din of the bombers. It was like movies of
wartime Japan. I looked up and there were planes bulging
with smoke.

The blue sky kept getting darker–
sometimes, I thought,
with your shadow.

In the end, I have a dog in my arms and a scarecrow for a
friend, but I never make it to Kansas. The field is wet and
stormy, I kiss three men goodnight for their magic. The
door to your childhood is opening for me. It allows me
passage into a brick wall, my fists full of shiny black
feathers, the shell of an egg, the howl of cold wind against
a mountain. Don't worry, your heart is in good hands. Let
me keep it a little longer; its blue glow illuminates
everything.

Aberrant Code V

I promised you a poem; I didn't say
it wouldn't be about me. In the end
I can only write myself into smaller circles.
On the internet you can pretend to be normal.
I can be a rock star and love parasailing.
Otherwise it's me and my stack of books,
my humming screens and the birds looking
curious into my window. They want in, want a hint
of my story. But I can't even give them that.
So many aberrations in my code, I can't tell you.
One story's about nuclear waste and the other a trick of genetics.
Either way the ground here is sown with monsters,
some of them weeping, some of them eating the furniture.

Girl with No Hands

She sits at a shrine, waiting for you
to reappear and claim her baby as your own,
no matter what lies you were told
about it being a monster.

Monster or demon, you told the messenger,
take good care of it until my return. You didn't know
what messages were interrupted, what lies
would tempt your mother to cast out

your wife and child, to a restless wilderness, she unable
to grasp fruit and berries in the woods,
unable to cradle your child. A flashback
to her fifteenth year, when her stepmother

persuaded her father to leave her on a mountain—
sleeping, handless, in a pool of blood. How you found her.
She weeps now, no father, no mother, no husband:
just the sound of the fountain and the coins

sleeping in the shade of a stone deity,
praying that, once more, she will be given
the snatch and grab, the fist, the noiseless fingertips.
You will rejoin her, embrace her, but she can only win

new precious hands in the sacred pool, her baby
slipping into the water as quietly as a stone.

In Phoenix, Heat Makes Us Chase Egrets

The ground here runs with quail and scrubby rabbits. We
pass acres of golf course where we chase a white egret,
that alien angel of swamps, from the quiet of its water
hazard.

The sand and sunlight are pink as raw skin and mesquite
wood burning on some grill blends with sweet Empress
trees reborn from scorched roots. Thorny acacias that
leans against me, arms menacing the sky.

One more dip in blue chlorine for you, while I open the
door to let out air conditioned frost and let in a snake that
curls up in your shoes. I eat soft prickly pear candy while
the mutated severed thumbs of Saguaro cacti hallucinate
the landscape, like Dali's chess set. They hide owls in the
holes of their skin.

The white egret circles
mini-malls, endlessly flees our arms
crying for forgotten water.

Waiting at the OB/Gyn's Office
For the Results of a Biopsy

How very pregnant all these women are.
Their husbands are nervous, sweaty
and excited. My husband holds my hand.

I tell him I am not like these other women,
proud of their swollen bellies and ankles;
I am here because I'm broken. I am half-joking.

I'm no older than these other women,
but half as hopeful. Even my palms feel
dry as sand. Every magazine reads "Parent," or "Child."

My follow-up visit will involve anesthesia
but no baby. Just cut and run.
I cannot smile back at the blonde beside me,

who keeps complaining she has to pee.
I slouch, keep my fists over my stomach.
All around me the baying of young. The doctor

is running behind. I read "What the Living Do."
My coat is pink wool today. I keep stroking it.
In ten more minutes they will read

the pieces of me
in a jar
like tea leaves.

Aberrant Code VI

What to expect? A misguided love interest,
a tragic disaster. One more lonely heart
echoing into the bluescreen. If I was a guitar
I'd be screaming for you. My teeth sunk into you.
Ten little bluebirds cry about the stains on their chests,
or was that the stain of dawn? All those gods
and flowers mixed up. We're good to go.
One suitcase of misgivings, one of dislocation.
We've traveled this path before, so don't expect a happy ending.
You, my friend, got your hopes up; keep to the root cellar,
that's where the truth lives, in the fingers of trees.
Your fingers like tree roots. Say goodbye to me
and my problems. Say hello to emblem and embrace.
Speak to me softly with the teeth of serpents.

The Tongue-Cut Sparrow's Song
For the Woodsman's Wife

You cut out my tongue because you were tired of your
husband waiting by the window. You begrudged me each
grain, each drop of water. What can you feed a bird that
cannot sing? What place does she have to hide? I even
bowed to you, bitter mistress, before your attack. What
harm could a sparrow do? Now you will see. If demons
rose around you like notes of my song, which did you not
earn?

In our world, birds
might become angels, or gods. Beware
the statue you do not feed.

The Woman Who Disappears

I died that night on the operating table.
It was not even childbirth—
just the scope, scalpel, balloon that did it,
my tissue so fragile the scrape, scrape
bled me to death.

I did not wake up with cramping,
infections and fevers.
My husband never drove me home,
stroking my hair, speaking softly.
I did not recover. And all my children were lost.

Here I am writing this poem as a ghost.
You cannot come looking for me;
if you put out a bucket for my spirit,
it will not fill with water.
If you pray to a tree, I will not arrive
with the feathers of a white bird.

Now I cannot save you. We put our lives
in the hands of others, and sometimes
they drop us like eggs. Our castles disappear,
and you will wonder, looking for us
in the islands of cranes.

See these wings? They are only
for the dead who try to rise again.

Awaré For the Woman Who Disappears
In Silence
— Based on "The Bush-Warbler's Home" and other stories

The Man chops wood for a living, yet still
gets lost in the forest. The woman appears,
surprises him. (You will know her by the flame
in the peony lantern,

the slim trunk of the green willows. Her hair falls
down her back like water.) Her splendid castle
amid the trees he has never seen before.
She is beautiful.

He bows down. She asks him to watch the castle,
to sweep the floor. Don't touch anything, don't go
exploring, she commands, and disappears. (She
is not what she seems.

She rules rivers, perhaps, or is truly a fox
spirit. How can he know?) He sweeps, obedient
for a time. He can't stop himself wandering
from room to room.

There are many treasures. He thinks he sees three
girls sweeping in a far room. They sing songs that
sound like wind through the pines. He touches things.
A nest with three eggs.

He drops them and hears a sorrowful cry, when
three small birds fly out a window. The rush of them
like spring. The woman returns, crying, how could you
lose me my daughters, no one is less trustworthy than a
human!

Before his eyes she becomes a bush-warbler,
bringer of spring, and flies away. For a hundred
years he stays, waiting,

in the castle, though it remains empty. He
touches nothing. In his dreams he marries her,
their three daughters sweep obediently.

Married Life

You sing in your sleep, he told her.
He rubs her stomach counter-clockwise.

Everyone says I'm lucky she says
to have you.

She washes his hair with lemon and chamomile
to make it more golden.

He chops vegetables on a wooden tablet he made himself.
She thinks she ought to be better with her hands.

You make my life easier she tells him.
I curse like a sailor since I met you he says.

Buyer's remorse? An empty cradle,
a woman sharper and shorter-haired than he'd married.

They break things made with care,
watch a pair of otters in the river

twisting and grooming and biting.
They look like they're trying to drown each other.

What do I sing? She asks him.
I don't know. I can't understand the words.

Snatches of song like you're underwater.
Sometimes, it sounds like you're laughing.

Anime Girls Consider the Resurrected

We are often the mouthpiece of resurrection—
Mary at the tomb,
Nausicaä buoyed by caterpillars
who bring her back to life on gold feelers.
Reanimated women with limbs of silver
and robots who house children's souls—
we all ache for this, the promised return.
The woman who disappears
must come back, in a bucket of water
at her brother's feet
or in the form of a white bird.
She does not stay away forever.

Part Five — When She Returns From the Floating World

"Our bodies may be transformed, but our lives will always be our own. We are birds who, though we may spit up blood, will go flying beyond the morning, on and on! To live is to change . . . "

—Princess Nausicaä, from the manga version of *Nausicaä of the Valley of the Wind,* volume 7, by Hayao Miyazaki

When the Bush-Warbler Returns

What happens to the bird
who keeps returning,
cooing to invisible hatchlings
in her empty nest?
She doesn't blame you
especially, but the way
she keep singing breaks your heart.
Isn't she the harbinger of spring,
now empty of eggs, of the hope
of changing seasons?
Too many times bringing string
home with nowhere to put it.
Too many feathers pulled
from her own coat
to line the home of no children.
Little bush-warbler,
whom we no longer name nightingale,
sing us a new song,
not of spring, of water,
of how we can make it alone
all those weary nights
and the moon so pregnant with light.

Don't Bring Me to the Fireworks,
The Fox-Wife Asks

They hurt my ears, make me run in circles. Under their
chemical light you might see my non-human face, the tail I
hide beneath skirts. In the city, under mercury vapor, you
never see me clearly.

I prefer the woods, the quiet howl of mosquitoes, of
cicadas. Build me a hut of mud where we never see the
stars, too bright. Bring me fans painted with cranes and
peonies, poetry folded into birds. Don't leave me in the
crowd, my nose assaulted by too many scents. Let us stay
far from others tonight, my love. Our celebrations will be
fur and paw, hand to chest. Let the fireworks with their
dizzy ghost spiders whine in the distance, keep me here,
bring me silk kimonos the color of bark and dirt to nest in.

Keep the copper smoke
and saltpeter, the dim trails
of chrysanthemums in the sky.

The Husband Tries to Write
To the Disappearing Wife

I could have kept you
in the palm of my hand,
but you weren't ready.

I know I have lost
your body, dissolved into
particles, swirling

like birdsong. I should
have known when I started
sweeping twigs and bits

of fur and feather
off our floors, when our baby
liked nothing better

than chewing beetles.
Our bargain was never strong
as straw, as autumn's

last light, easily
shattered. Why is it I want
to carve you into

my palm, from pain
into memory, that I sit up
night after night

recreating—first,
the moon and moth, the white shrine—
your eyes, too bright

to be human. The songs
I write start with your hair but

end with your heart.

No poetry seems right
without your crooked smile.
Without the scrape

of your sharp teeth
against my lips, there is
no word for kiss.

Why We Cannot Have Children

Because I am a witch, a demon.

Because one might be born with a fox's tail, or a white
bird's feathers.

Because our children would all become monsters.

Because I would rather not pass on the problems coded
within me.

Because although I love you we cannot produce viable
offspring, like hybridized tomatoes or peaches.

Because my name is whispering creek and yours is sky writing.

Because I was born in the wrong season, the season of
changelings.

Because while you sleep I become my true self, my animal
nature.

Because you would not like the land of my birth.

Because I go where you cannot follow.

The Animal Heart: She Warns Him

Don't come too near; you might see light glistening off
white fangs, a white underbelly. A woman doesn't fight
like that, you say, and then notice the claw, the tail in the
half-moon. Kits running around your ankles. Beware the
woman you meet on the path at night; don't look in her
eyes. She could be *tanuki*, if she has far-set eyes with
shadows, or *kitsune*, close-set eyes and high cheekbones.
Sometimes you have called us prostitutes, left money at
the shrine after a night with us. But we are not after
money, and you will go home betrayed with fur on your
clothing and leaf-mold on your breath. Don't be surprised
at the trail of blood on our doorstep. A frightening
vision—you trusted her docile nature would protect you,
that you could inflict harm without being harmed? I don't
carry a fan, but a scrap of sharpened stick, and if you
follow a flame into the forest, what can you expect?

When I shed my skin
for you, I left intact
my animal heart

the desire to crack bones between delicate teeth.

On the Full Moon

You didn't understand
        why I fainted in your arms–
            the moon's pull too

The Fox-Wife's Husband Considers
The Warning Signs

When you were pregnant, you didn't just crave dirt and
ice, but grasshoppers, field mice, frogs.

When you had our baby, I caught you licking his head
absently on more than one occasion.

Sometimes when you thought you were alone, you gnawed
on your forearm.

You kept a collection of bones in the house.

Maybe I wanted to see you another way. Maybe I missed
the clues on purpose.

Until now, I wasn't looking for evidence. Until now, I
hadn't thought of you as different, as separate. But now
you are gone, there is no denying it; I thought you were
part of me but really you were something else entirely.

Amaterasu, the Sun Goddess, Returns

I went underground to escape
(my brother, the storm)
breaking everything
(the way he does)
his fists everywhere.
I hid there, taking the warmth
of my breath, my gold fingers.

The people mourned,
tried to lure me from the cave,
but I was happy in the quiet
damp dark, sleeping.
Then there was dancing,
goddesses singing my name,
throwing clothes and pride to the wind
and then laughter, surprising, my own.
My laughter filling the cave until
I joined them,
naked in the light,
unable to resist the shocking,
unstoppable song of our bodies.

What I Bring Back From Japan

I fling myself
into the arms of your stories,
Japan, beautiful island of cranes
and peony lanterns, the blush
of cherry blossoms continually fading.

What *kami*-spirits will you send
to hold me here
floating above you
listening to the songs of your bush-warblers and swallows,
the rustling bamboo and camphor tree?

When I return, will I recognize myself
laughing in the shadow of caves
wearing the disguise of a white bird?

Extinguish

That last night
we stayed at The Chrysalis.

In all the pictures, part of me
strays the frame—
a leg, an arm, the top of my head.

It was October, the trees were bright,
the endless fields full of pumpkin, apples.

How could we know that after this
the smell of smoke would linger
in our heads? Even then I felt
my hands curling.

Our time together finite,
a ribbon of paper burning.

At the end, what the flame leaves:
a white flash beneath eyelids,
charred dust of moth wings,

the inward turn of the body
from flesh to ash.

The Note the Fox-Wife Leaves Him

You didn't know
I was happier in the dirt
before this terrible skin, its senses,
before the dread of waking every day to me,
to you. This isn't what I knew before,
the air and light. Heavier, and darker
than I expected, not just the body,
my mind—remembrances hang
in the trees like ghosts, every glen
a graveyard. You don't know what satisfies—
maybe my heart was hungrier than this.

And when I leave you behind
whatever I become next
will be better. I know it.
Don't come looking for me,
I don't want to be found.
The next life for me
must, must be what I've hoped for.
I shed claws and wings once already;
don't think it won't be easier
to shed this, where the cling
and thrum of gristle and blood
grow so faint I forget them.

What Was Lost

You think because the bush-warbler
sings in the plum tree,
because the red elk returns to the forest,
that I will return to you?
The flowers, the rain, the trees may return,
the dead trunk may bloom,
and the little rabbit and the fox return—
but not I, not to you.

I am the daughter of the sun,
I will stay in my cave
until my own laughter drives me out.
Rest your hands on the door,
on the window, let your eyes search
the sky for the white arm, the hair
like a dark wing against you.
Listen: at night the spirits call to the earth
and you call to me. Only the earth
will answer.

Half-Life

After you leave the hospital
the sky a disrespectful blaze of blue
white birds fly overhead

a shimmer you can barely make out
egrets? snow geese? tundra swans?
their uneven V

illegible in the blue sky
like a signature you misread
at the doctor's office.

She Returns to the Floating World

Last night I dreamed I was a firefly,
and you shook a stick at me.

I was a peony flower, my feet in the mud,
and you put me in a vase to wither.

I was a white butterfly, and your relatives
shooed me from your deathbed.

All these years ago you promised me
you'd tend to my grave, be faithful.

I promised I'd return to you,
and I kept my promise.

Now, when I look in your face,
you do not know me.

I keep resurfacing, hoping one day
you will know my name.

She Returns to the Floating World II

When she came back from the dead, she wasn't the same.
You knew she couldn't be. In her eyes something,
but her mouth couldn't form the words.
Her body wouldn't stay still—in your grasp
she seemed to be one thing, then another.
She simply couldn't speak
in the same voice. Her bones dissolved in her sleep,
her blood angry ran in many directions.
When you looked at her too long she shimmered.
You couldn't be sure she was even there,
maybe she wanted the sleep. You worry she's lying to you.
You worry that however long you have her,
the grave will always have more.
She came back to you, again and again,
always wearing a new skin.
If they planted you in the ground, you don't know
if you would have the strength to rise again.

She Returns to the Floating World III

You have to be more than human to begin with.
Renewal takes time, spirit and sinew.
These bright containers are temporary.
Every turtle-princess, every peony-girl,
knows beneath the surface of the water is another world.
I was in danger, and you could not save me.
You are in danger. I am danger. If you hold my hand,
you will disappear leaving flames in your wake.
You may return in a hundred years
holding a treasure chest full of demons and lost time.
I promised you nothing except remembrance.

Anxiety, Post-Apocalyptic Futures, Whatever:
A New Song

I knew we were tired of looking at mushroom clouds in the ceiling tiles, tired of robots replacing our arms with metal rods. It was time again to call out in the darkness, tidings of gladness. In one hand I hid apples; in another, pieces of eight. We were left alone with barely any time. One night I crept into the cavern where a boy lay with a wool blanket wrapped around his torso. He looked so real, sleeping there, I almost touched his eyelashes. The cave was full of coughing, this time the tirade was real, the plague unanswerable by human tongues. In a bag are a pair of mittens, still tied together, a pair of tongs, and a chemical hotplate. One bottle of grapeseed oil, another of goat's milk.

Were there flowers
or were there only
cracks in the glass?

Only the toadstools know for sure. Once we prayed to the gleaming red eyes of the machine, once we spoke in code and knew our paths were righteous. But now, now, only sticks and stones are left and we are tired of all the breaking. Whatever language, we are asking for praise, for freedom in the cornfields, for the rebirth of the sun.

Goodbye Farewell Goodnight
Oyasuminasai Ja-ne Sayonara

Learning to let go of me
letting go of my body
a certain form
quick and transient as frost as smoke as vapor
nothing you can trust
and like you this life has not been easy
on anyone
I'm sorry I didn't turn out
like you expected
sorry the last sight you'll see is the flash of silver in the sky
and that is it
a flurry of leaves and dust
I'm sorry I couldn't stay couldn't make us a family
couldn't be the one to save you
couldn't hold myself here I had to say goodbye
like the cherry blossoms already browning on the grass
like the dogwood already curling their thin petals in the light
tough as rice paper
strong as the peony petal
hard as the willow branch
I wanted to be sturdy I wanted more I wanted you
but instead I have the transitive the shift the loss the
goodbye farewell goodnight
the moon comes out to say it for me
scratches the meanings into the shadows of the hallway
with more light you might have seen me turn
transitory transition translation transient
to keep me here would mean to burn me in effigy
the stiff sharp charrings more permanent than I could ever be

The Little Mermaid Has No Regrets

In the end, I wanted to wake up sea foam.
I didn't want these legs anymore that carry me
uselessly from house to house, searching for lost love.
I wore dresses that covered up the pale lengths,
in sea greens and azure blues, wove seashells into hair
and sang on a rock. None of it did any good.

Once, I would have died for you. I changed, I did,
and all for just one kiss, one touch. Should it have burned
so much? I miss cool scales, the constant wet embrace,
the skittering across tips of tsunami. While you
were out catching fish, with your tangled nets,
I was watching, wishing for a different body, one to
entangle you.

It never did me any good. So I will wait for the ocean's promise:
that once again I will end up on this beach, disintegrate,
spatter away into the essences of salt, sand, earth.
A waste of skin and scale, but at least once again
I will be part of the dance, the maternal water
carrying me home.

Autobiography I

No, last time you read me
wrong. I'm not the main character,
I'm the photographer, the one
with her feet in the river.
I'm the frame of reference,
not the delicate willow branch,
not fragile and crumpled as a peony.
You mistook me for the love interest
in a bunny suit, or read me as the robot
But I am neither. Here my abode is stump, moss;
I am stronger. The wind
can't kill me now. I leave town
and you won't hear from me again.
Stop imagining I was waiting
for your permission.
I started this before you even knew me.
It's not what you think.
The story doesn't end.
One more time the dust off the
butterfly wing leads to spring.

Autobiography II

After she vanishes, after you've
already written her off,
she is reborn, each time
less likely to know the tongues
of insects, more likely to smell blood.
This time, she'll be tumbling
through a metal tube wearing platinum
armor, armed with a crossbow,
her hair in a Joan-of-Arc bob
framing the scene.
Don't be surprised;
the woman reappears
and this time, she will be a stranger to you;
this time, she will keep more to herself.

Yume (The Dream)

I hold a small animal in my hands. I do not know its name,
but I hear what it whispers to me—something about
whiteness, a weeping cherry—another word for brightness,
and yet a third for how hard we hold on to what must
disappear. I lean to the animal with my cheek, and it
nibbles my brown hair. By now it is sunset, in winter, the
sky like iced concrete, the wind is pulling me over,
bending toward the ground.

Tell me, what direction
to point my nose
towards spring?

Which way to fly towards what is new again? But the
animal doesn't answer. It keeps circling round, frantic, as
if its movements are a calendar I might live by. When I
open a door, the light is gone, the world around me has
gone black, and the balloon waiting to take me home has
toppled. All I am left with are these empty hands and no
direction. I was hoping for a prayer, but here all I find is
absence.

The Fox-Wife's Invitation

These ears aren't to be trusted. The keening in the night,
didn't you hear? Once I believed all the stories didn't have
endings, but I realized the endings were invented, like
zero, had yet to be imagined. The months come around
again, and we are in the same place; full moons, cherries in
bloom, the same deer, the same frogs, the same helpless
scratching at the dirt. You leave poems I can't read behind
on the sheets, I try to teach you songs made of twigs and
frost. You may be imprisoned in an underwater palace, and
I'll come riding to the rescue in disguise. You leave the
magic tricks to me and to the teakettle. I've inhaled the
spells of willow trees, spat them out as blankets of white
crane feathers. Sleep easy.

From behind the closet door
I'll invent our fortunes, spin them
from my own skin.

Notes on Poems

"The Fox-Wife Dreams"
Based on the Japanese folk tale about the *kitsune*, a fox-turned-woman, who marries a human man, one of many such stories about transforming wives.

The entire story that was quoted for Section I can be found here:
http://www.big.or.jp/~loupe/links/etale3.shtml

"Crane Wife"
Based on the Japanese fairy tale of the same name.

"An American Love Letter to Hayao Miyazaki"
Hayao Miyazaki, the famous Japanese director and producer of animated films, was born the same year as my father, in 1941. A *phurba* was a type of dagger-like instrument with religious significance in Shinto and Buddhist practices. A *kami* is a ghost or spirit.

"The Princess Who Loved Insects"
This poem is based on the 12th century story, "Tsutsumi Chunagon Monogatari." Although dragons are more common in Chinese art than Japanese art, in Japanese paintings from the 12th-17th century, dragons were often painted in bodies of water to represent the spirit of the sea, river, or lake.

"Big Sister, Little Brother"
This poem is based on two Japanese folk tales of the same name.

"White Bird Sister"
Based on the Japanese fairy tale of the same name.

"Standing in the Anime Kingdom"
Otaku is a semi-derogatory term—an American slang equivalent might be "fanboy" or "fangirl."

"Little Girls, Atom Bombs"
This poem refers to images from Hayao Miyazaki's music video for the song "On Your Mark."

"A Grownup Considers the Spiritual Themes of a Children's Movie"
This poem references Hayao Miyazaki's film for children, "My Neighbor Totoro," about a benign nature spirit who watches over two girls while their mother is in the hospital. The poem also contains a line from the book of Isaiah and several from Psalm 73.

"The Fire of Foxes"
The first section of this poem refers to a section of Judges 15: "So Samson . . . caught three hundred foxes . . . and he turned them tail to tail, and put a torch between each pair of tails. And when he had set fire to the torches, he let the foxes go into the standing grain of the Philistines, and burned . . . " The second section refers to a well-known folk tale of Japan, sometimes called "The Burning Rice Field."

"Green Willow Wife"
From the Japanese fairy tale, "Green Willow."

"The Tongue-Cut Sparrow's Song for the Woodsman's Wife"
Based on the famous Japanese fairy tale, "The Tongue-Cut Sparrow."

"Awaré for the Woman who Disappears in Silence"
According to Hayao Kawai in *The Japanese Psyche: Major Motifs in the Fairy Tales of Japan*, *awaré* means "softly despairing sorrow."

"She Returns to the Floating World"
"Ukiyo" is the Japanese word for the concept of "The Floating World," which is sometimes associated with prostitution and red-light districts, and sometimes with a pleasure-seeking lifestyle. The floating world is also associated with the subconscious and dreams in folk tales.
Notes on animal names:

"Tanuki" is sometimes mistranslated as "badger," but is really a species commonly called a "raccoon-dog" that closely resembles a large raccoon.

The "bush-warbler" was often called a "Japanese nightingale" in Western translations of fairy tales, and was a traditional harbinger of spring.

"Uzura" is a seasonal word in Japanese poetry, which means "quail."

"I deeply admire the skill with which Jeannine Hall Gailey weaves myth and folklore into poems illuminating the realities of modern life. Gailey is, quite simply, one of my favorite American poets; and *She Returns to the Floating World* is her best collection yet."
> —Terri Windling, writer, editor, and artist (editor, *The Year's Best Fantasy and Horror* series and collections like *The Armless Maiden*, as well as *The Endicott Studio*)

"Kin to the extraordinary pillow book of tenth-century Japanese court poet Sei Shōnagon, Jeannine Hall Galley has created her own collection of extraordinary myths, fables, and folktales for the twenty-first century . Fed by scholarship, a passion for Anime, and a singular, brilliant imagination, this poet designs female heroes who challenge and transform our quotidian lives."
> —Sandra Alcosser, author of *Except by Nature*

"The poems in Gailey's highly anticipated second collection mesmerize the reader with its glimmering revisitations of myth that explore love and desire via the most unexpected conduits: foxes, robots, and the "kingdom of Anime."*She Returns to the Floating World* is a captivating gathering of poems written with the rare but immense knowledge of (the) matters of the heart and the often-ecstatic natural world. Gailey illuminates our place within myth with stunning precision and the awareness of what it really means to be fully alive with the ones you love."
> —Aimee Nezhukumatathil, author of *At the Drive-in Volcano*

"These poems fuse figures and narratives from Japanese myths and folklore, Shinto spirits, philosophy and popular culture to explore the nexus between the spiritual and the sensual, places where the act of touching is both metaphorical and sometimes violently, painfully physical. Amid musings on the darker corners of Japan's postwar legacy are flashes of the humor born of perseverance. Even Godzilla has a cameo."
—Roland Kelts, *Japanamerica*

ABOUT JEANNINE HALL GAILEY

Jeannine Hall Gailey is the former Poet Laureate of Redmond, Washington and she is the author of three books of poetry, *Becoming the Villainess*, *She Returns to the Floating World*, and *Unexplained Fevers*. Her work has been featured on NPR's The Writers Almanac with Garrison Keillor and Verse Daily, and was included in *The Year's Best Fantasy and Horror*. Journals her poems have appeared in include *The American Poetry Review*, *Prairie Schooner*, and *The Iowa Review*.

She has published reviews and interviews in *The Rumpus*, *Poets & Writers* web site, and The Poetry Foundation web site. She was awarded the Dorothy Sargent Rosenberg Prize in 2007 and 2011 and won a Washington State Artist Trust GAP grant for work on this book.

Jeannine is a comic book and anime fan who studied biology before her graduate studies in creative writing. She volunteers as an editorial consultant for Crab Creek Review and teaches part-time at National University's MFA program.

Visit her website at: www.webbish6.com

Made in the USA
San Bernardino, CA
28 September 2016